THIS IS ME! 2022

WORD WEAVERS

Edited By Allie Jones

First published in Great Britain in 2022 by:

Young Writers
Remus House
Coltsfoot Drive
Peterborough
PE2 9BF
Telephone: 01733 890066
Website: www.youngwriters.co.uk

Printed and bound in the UK by BookPrintingUK
Website: www.bookprintinguk.com
YB0505Y

FOREWORD

For Young Writers' latest competition This Is Me, we asked primary school pupils to look inside themselves, to think about what makes them unique, and then write a poem about it! They rose to the challenge magnificently and the result is this fantastic collection of poems in a variety of poetic styles.

Here at Young Writers our aim is to encourage creativity in children and to inspire a love of the written word, so it's great to get such an amazing response, with some absolutely fantastic poems. It's important for children to focus on and celebrate themselves and this competition allowed them to write freely and honestly, celebrating what makes them great, expressing their hopes and fears, or simply writing about their favourite things. This Is Me gave them the power of words. The result is a collection of inspirational and moving poems that also showcase their creativity and writing ability.

I'd like to congratulate all the young poets in this anthology, I hope this inspires them to continue with their creative writing.

CONTENTS

Mia Templar (10)	82
Lexie Crawford (10)	84
Sam Thwaites (10)	86
Andrew Thompson (10)	88
Georgia Hodge (10)	90
Kaiden Moffat (10)	92
Jack Cornwall (11)	94
Oscar Stewart (10)	96
Amy Lockhart (10)	98
Lily Forbes (10)	100
Isabella Chen (10)	102
Kayla Grieve (10)	104
Millie Hinton (10)	106
Anna Jackson (10)	108
Molly McElroy (10)	110
Max Ross (10)	112
Erin Perry (10)	114
Nancy Mould (10)	116
Nathan Neve (10)	118
Samuel Wells (10)	120
Alfie Barnes (10)	122
Emma Thompson (10)	124
Oliwia Wleklinska (10)	125
Elizabeth Flynn (10)	126
Eilidh McAleese (10)	127
Charlie Penny (10)	128
Jamie Drummond (10)	129
Logan Wallace (10)	130

Pantside Primary School, Newbridge

Mia Booton (8)	131
Layla May Fritter (10)	132
Kira Taylor (11)	133
Shane Thomas (9)	134
Emily Rush (10)	135
Peyton Beach (8)	136
Logan Roscoe (9)	137
Nathan Carless (7)	138
Jayden Manning (11)	139
Harrison Brown (8)	140
Kai Davies (10)	141
Carys Jones (9)	142

Ruby-Rose Martin (9)	143
Amy Smith (11)	144
Shay Mason (11)	145
Oscar Lewis-Gamble (7)	146
Skye Dugmore (7)	147
Brooke Kavanagh (11)	148
Casey Jones (10)	149
Marcus Phillips (10)	150
Tylan Davies (9)	151
Harvey Thomas John Price (9)	152
Talisha Hughes (9)	153
Corey Bennett (8)	154
Kaiden Wheeler (8)	155
Joseph John (7)	156
Eliza Bennett (9)	157
Myles Challenger (8)	158
Denni Roberts (8)	159

Pardes House Primary School, Finchley

Daniel Bordon (9)	160
Yitzi Raymond (10)	162
Avi Schleider (10)	164
Avraimy Cutler (9)	165
Daniel Bude (10)	166
Yissochor Moller (10)	167
Yossef Besnainou (10)	168
Yisroel Gurvits (10)	169
Sruli Springer (8)	170
Ashi Kraus (9)	171
Yosef Elmkies (8)	172
Rephael Hakkak (9)	173
Yoni Hoffman (9)	174
Rafi Miller (9)	175
Zvi Gutfreund (9)	176
Ben Friedman (10)	177
Ben Spitzer (9)	178
Oshi Levy (10)	179
Eli Mordfield (9)	180
Chaim Ackerman (10)	181
Dovid Greenberg (10)	182
Ariel Weissbraun (9)	183
Aaron Winegarten (8)	184

Kovi Diamant (8)	185
Shimeon Israeli (8)	186
Tuvia Deutsch (8)	187
Yossi Werjuka (9)	188
Sruli Hackenbroch (9)	189
Ari Lerch (10)	190
Raphael Posen (8)	191
Avi Kahan (8)	192
Izy Benaim (8)	193

St Martin's School, Mill Hill

Amar Madahar (7)	194
Chloe Barber (11)	196
Olivia Wilson (10)	197

St Mary's RC Primary School, Lowestoft

Poppy Webb (11)	198
Baikey Hou (10)	199

Thameside Primary School, Caversham

Maia Magson (9)	200
Evie Titchener (9)	201
Eason Wu (9)	202
Rose Higley (10)	203
Aadhya Shukla (9)	204
Hannah Spencer (10)	205
Deanne Gyeni (10)	206
Saida Rahman	207
Indi Holland (9)	208
Ernie Owens (9)	209
Nadia Ouadahi (9)	210
Phoebe Hinchmore (10)	211
Mary Mackinnon (9)	212
Ben Martin (9)	213
Tamzin Biddle (10)	214
Yavuz Selim Baydu (9)	215
Roman Bosklopper (10)	216
Jaide Thompson (10)	217
Grace Hilden	218

Jake Mackrory (9)	219
Barney Grace (10)	220
Hessah Alhouti (9)	221

THE POEMS

This Is Me

When I cry my river flows fast,
But I shed tears of joy remembering the past.

When I feel small the trees lose their leaves,
A 10-year-old boy who just wants to please.

When I feel sad my flowers fill with gloom,
But when I feel happy they will bloom.

When I am angry it is a big earthquake,
But I will always stop when chocolate is at stake.

When I feel empty I feel out of place,
When others are proud pride beams on my face.

But when I am lonely, I don't feel like me,
I am always loved by my family.

But it does not matter how I feel because I know
my feelings are real,
I want to feel like I am me,
My parents always make me be me.

Leo Barry (10)
All Souls' Catholic Primary School, Chapelfields

This Is Me!

People say I'm funny,
I don't always agree,
Although I breeze through books,
I get too engrossed in expectation and reality,
But I can paint my toes and prance around
gracefully,
I fall and cry and believe I'm not good enough,
Black's my favourite colour, the colour of death,
I have lost someone who's great and I worry who's
next,
Peacefully I listen to music and draw how I feel,
I don't always get time to myself because growing
up is tough,
A good friend I am to others,
I worry day and night if they think I'm good
enough,
Many things I do, dancing, tennis, football, guitar
and more,
I feel pressure on my shoulders - can I take much
more?
Yet, when I feel sad and want to hide away,
Somewhere in the darkness, this tiny volcano is
waiting to show everyone its full eruption.

That's me, Tessa, standing tall,
I have my ups and downs, but nevertheless,
I stand on this mountain of joy in my black dress,
Ready for anything,
That puts me to the test.

Tessa Baker (11)
All Souls' Catholic Primary School, Chapelfields

This Is Me

I enjoy doing art, I love to run,
I'm good at maths,
I am a good son,
I give lots of laughs,
I've got a twin sister,
I'm scared of dogs,
When I play football I might come out with a blister,
I am quite smart,
I love to have fun,
In summer I love to play in the sun,
I build Lego as it is my hobby,
My favourite Harry Potter character is Dobby,
I am short, could it be?
This is what I'm like as I am me,
I'm good at spelling,
But no good at yelling,
I like some animals,
I am helpful and truthful,
So that is all about me!

Roman Wale (10)
All Souls' Catholic Primary School, Chapelfields

All About Me!

My dream is to become a nursery teacher,
I enjoy reading, writing, baking and singing,
I'ma sister, a daughter and a good helper!
I look forward to what the future will bring.

I am a caring Catholic that's always ready to help,
I play piano and have a big imagination,
I am courageous and funny without a doubt,
I complete my work with concentration.

My favourite colours are blue, purple and red,
I like to play on my iPad and eat food,
After a long day I can't wait to go to bed,
Listening to music puts me in a good mood.

Annabelle Tarpey (11)
All Souls' Catholic Primary School, Chapelfields

This Is Me!

To create me you will need:
A slab of books
A hot grilled pizza
A pinch of kindness and happiness
A sprinkle of intelligence
15kg of fun and flowers
A sprinkle of netball and horse riding
A pinch of animal lover

Now you need to:
Add one hot grilled pizza
Mix with the slab of books roughly
Add a pinch of kindness and happiness
A sprinkle of intelligence
15kg of fun and flowers
A sprinkle of netball and horse riding
Lastly, the pinch of animal lover and...

This is me!

Julia Podolanczuk (10)
All Souls' Catholic Primary School, Chapelfields

My Colours

I'm kind and calm, just like pink,
Me and my dog, we've got a real link.
Eloquent and truthful, just like purple,
Just because I'm truthful doesn't mean I'm gullible.
Funny and loyal, just like blue,
I've got three pets, not just two.
I'm loud like orange, but quiet like peach,
I'm tall like green and I've got big feet.
I can be angry like red, but I always calm down,
I'm warm like yellow, but cold like cyan.
These are my true colours and they make me, me!

Ffion West (11)
All Souls' Catholic Primary School, Chapelfields

This Is Me

Patrick's my name
Ya lookin' kinda lame!
Let's play a game

Patrick! Patrick!
He smashed a dish!
But still he isn't some sort of big pink fat starfish!

Cousin to many
He's good on the telly
If he went on a gameshow
He wouldn't be lame though

Yeah! Me and the boys in the back
Chilling, Fortnite, a weird sort of hack
Winning! Got the dub with the gold tack
Watching! TV has got some Jack Black!

Patrick Ceairns (10)
All Souls' Catholic Primary School, Chapelfields

This Is Me!

To create me you will need:
An encyclopedia of knowledge; I love to find out facts,
A sprinkle of intelligence,
A bowlful of vegetables with gravy,
A spoonful of speed,
A tub of hunger.

Now you need to:
Heat a large bowl of boiling water,
Throw the encyclopedia into it,
Then sprinkle the intelligence and mix it with the veg,
Pour the tub of hunger into the bowl,
Add the speed and leave to boil for two hours.

This is me.

James Murphy (11)
All Souls' Catholic Primary School, Chapelfields

The Perfect Person

The left ear of a jolly jaguar.
A bowl of fur from a rock-climbing cat.
A planet's water supply worth of wackiness.
A jar of lightning from a country of creativity.
The bright blue minerals from the caverns of
curiosity.
A flask of snot from the lion of love.
The biggest scale from the back of a sneaky snake.
A truckload of Tommy.

This is the recipe for a portion of Tommy.
Drink it to become the best version of me!

Tommy Wheeler (10)
All Souls' Catholic Primary School, Chapelfields

This Is Me

My name is K to the ee to the g-a-n,
I do like games but I'm not about the fame,
I do like food, but not when I'm in a mood,
I do like sleeping, but not when I'm weeping,
I do like football and animals too,
When I dream I theme,
Brother of many, I like watching telly,
I have brown eyes and brown hair too,
And guess what? This is me, dude!

Keegan Biggs (11)
All Souls' Catholic Primary School, Chapelfields

A Milkshake Of Me

To make me you will need the following:
Half a cup of mushed brain,
A cup full of swimming water,
A sprinkle of sad particles,
More than enough happy,
Crushed up book pages,
A bowl of responsibility,
Cut up gymnastic mats,
Pink powder for my favourite colour,
And liquified thorns to represent our Lord, our
Catholicity.

You made me!

Lily Wale (10)
All Souls' Catholic Primary School, Chapelfields

This Is Me

An ordinary girl who's proud and wise
With black hair and dark brown eyes
I can hear God's call wanting me to be
An interior designer full of love and glee
I travel to church as a disciple of our Lord
To spread the word and help faith be restored
But there is one thing that makes me different from the rest
To always be me, I try my best.

Maria Rabvukwa (11)
All Souls' Catholic Primary School, Chapelfields

This Is Me!

When I am upset, I'm like an empty cloud,
But when I'm filled with joy, the sun's shining
bright.
I like to listen to the nice music sounds,
I am a Catholic and I can see God's light.
I have loving parents and three great brothers.
In school, I'm an amazing friend to others!

Alicja Wegrzyniak (10)
All Souls' Catholic Primary School, Chapelfields

How To Make Me

To make me you will need the following:

Blue powder for my favourite colour blue.
A teaspoon of French, Irish and English blood.
Dead clownfish mashed into pieces to add a bit of funny.
Spiders' eyes for poor eyesight.
A jug of responsibility.
And finally the anti-school virus.

Etienne Ouillon (10)
All Souls' Catholic Primary School, Chapelfields

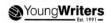

This Is Who I Am

An intelligent mathematician,
I have an undying passion for baking,
A devastating sucker for endless fun,
There is nothing I wouldn't love making,
I would like to try garden raking,
An engineer has always been my dream job,
I would like to have a good corn on the cob!

Nathan Adebote (11)
All Souls' Catholic Primary School, Chapelfields

This Is Me

N O A H
That's my name
I play games
I'm only ten
At least I don't sit on the wall of shame!

I am big
I am not thick
I don't play with a stick

I'm a brother
Not a sister
I'm a footballer
Not a burger lover!

Noah Meehan (10)
All Souls' Catholic Primary School, Chapelfields

This Is Me!

Ireland
Scotland
Wales
England too
Maths is what I love to do!

Helpful
Competitive
That's what I am
Believing in God is where it began.

God is life
God is Earth
To Heaven I follow
My faith will show.

Lottie Ward (11)
All Souls' Catholic Primary School, Chapelfields

This Is Me!

Dinosaurs,
Yeah, football too,
They are what I love to do.
Hardcore Irish,
I'm also stylish.
Not the blondest, but I am quite cool,
And you know what? I'm good in the pool.
I'm a great old athlete,
This rap is now complete!

James Clancy (11)
All Souls' Catholic Primary School, Chapelfields

This Is Me!

I am an enthusiastic learner,
I love to play badminton,
I am a happy helper,
I am a loving son,
I am an early waker,
I love to watch television,
I am a wide smile,
I am a forgiving person,
I am unique,
And this is me!

Jacob Bennett (10)
All Souls' Catholic Primary School, Chapelfields

This Is Me

I am a boy who,
Is always keeping active,
And loves playing sports.

I like to do maths,
So I can figure stuff out,
And I'm interested.

I love rugby,
When I play I play with passion,
Synergy is key.

Ted White (11)
All Souls' Catholic Primary School, Chapelfields

This Is Me

D o love my food
A nd animals too, especially rabbits
N ever sad, always happy
C aring, loving, I love theatre craft
E ating pasta and pizza too
R osey and Posey love me lots.

Catherine Towey (10)

All Souls' Catholic Primary School, Chapelfields

This Is Me

I am a...
Kind helper
Swimming superstar
Dog adorer
Loving person
Good gamer
Maths solver
Positive child
Light sleeper
And finally...
Hard-working being.

Riley Pattison (10)
All Souls' Catholic Primary School, Chapelfields

This Is Me!

One Sunday morning I wake and see
The sun rising up for me
I put on my trainers, ready for a run
In the sun
Even when I ache
I drink a hot choc with a Flake
The tastiest lunch I love the most
It's got to be beans on toast
After all of that, what I need is a chillax
I sit with a blanket to rest to the max
Oh no, whoops, my homework I forgot
There's probably a lot!
My reading comprehension
I must give it my attention
Time for a film, I'm watching Harry Potter
I don't like Draco Malfoy, he's a rotter
Time for tea, then off to bed
And rest my sleepy head!

Naomie White (7)

Handforth Grange Primary School, Handforth

Blue

A wolf called Blue
Had six puppies but no food.
Blue approached me with her tail between her legs.
I could see she was hungry and her eyes full of dread.
She was scared to approach me, but approach me she did.
She asked me for my help to feed her kids.
She was an old wolf, her puppies were young of age... But the power of hope and strength helped her to be brave.
She now visits every night to show her respect - To say thank you to a stranger, she will never forget.

Parris Dickson (9)
Handforth Grange Primary School, Handforth

All About Me

A lthough an unusual name, named after

T he great goddess of wisdom

H owever, not all that meets the eye

E very way, I am creative and funny

N ow that's not all, I love history, art and music in school

A nd I love to play with my friends

L ucky for me I have five pets: a cat, two guinea pigs and two snakes

U nbelievably

C reative

Y oung heart forever.

Athena Lucy Morrissey (9)

Handforth Grange Primary School, Handforth

I Am Unique

M e, Chloe, Mummy, Daddy and Fudge are my family.

I am quite shy, though I

L ove playing with my friends: Kayla, Alfie and Holly.

W henever a pen is near, I grab it and start to draw -

A nd when I get the opportunity I dance and dance!

R eading is one of my favourite pastimes.

D rama, English and art compete, I just can't choose.

I am completely unique.

Hannah Milward (9)
Handforth Grange Primary School, Handforth

Gymnastics Is Me

G ymnastics is me
Y ou always try your best
M ounting the beam, you never have a rest
N ever give up because practice makes perfect
A crobatic flips
S wing on the bars like a monkey
T umbling on the springy floor
I nteresting somersaults
C artwheeling around
S plits and straddle

B ritish
G ymnastics is me!

Ava-Rose Ogunyemi (8)

Handforth Grange Primary School, Handforth

This Is Me

Well, my name is Ellie,
And I love watching telly.
It's not all that I do,
I go paddleboarding too.
I rock climb on a wall,
And for my age I am quite tall.
I ride my bike with my dad,
Who sometimes gets mad.
We like eating chocolate together till late.
I love riding my bike,
But it's not all that I like.
I like walking with my family,
It makes me feel lovely.

Ellie McGrath (8)
Handforth Grange Primary School, Handforth

I Am A Rainbow

R ed is my favourite me, a happy, cheerful, loving me

A nxious is my worrying me, but only when I'm scared

I am very brave, I want to give everything a go

N iamh is my name, I am colourful and bright

B lue is my excited me, when I jump around and play

O range is my kind me, I am helpful to my friends

W arner is my family name, we are happy every day.

Niamh Warner (8)
Handforth Grange Primary School, Handforth

My World Of Wonder

A world full of joy and happiness,
That is my world of wonder,
A world full of joy and peace,
A place beyond your wildest dreams,
This is my world of wonder,
A place where I am never sad,
I know I will always be glad,
In my world of wonder,
I can choose what I am,
I can choose what I can be,
It is my life, it is my destiny,
This is me,
In my world of wonder.

Jamie-Leigh Needham (9)
Handforth Grange Primary School, Handforth

The Beginning

All my life I've been me
But what is me? We shall see
I have dreams and I have hope
Just like you and any folk
One day I will be a karate black belt
Getting belts is the best I've felt
One day I hope to help us all
By using what I've learnt in school
Together we'll make the world great
That's the future, I can't wait.

Bramwell Crumpton-Taylor (7)
Handforth Grange Primary School, Handforth

This Is Me And My Dream

T his is me and all about my dream
H ello I say to everyone I meet
I n this poem it is all about me
S o, my idol I look up to, who is he?

I love him and his name is Ronnie
S uiii he says, suiii Ronaldo I look up to you

M y poem has come to an end
E ven try to make your idol your friend.

Will Jones (10)
Handforth Grange Primary School, Handforth

Astronaut

A n astronaut I wish to be
S eeing the whole solar system
T o orbit the sun would take 365 days
R ushing comets and shooting stars as fast as a rocket
O rbiting the sun
N eil Armstrong was the first person on the moon
A steroids catching fire
U nknown universe
T o go to space is my dream.

Zoi Tsiavo (9)

Handforth Grange Primary School, Handforth

My Hobby Of History

Hi, I'm Ivars
I have a hobby of history
If I enjoy it
You should too
What was the first jet?
The Germans made it
The Me 262!
What was the RAF's best plane?
The Spitfire of course!
Ask me any question
I will tell you
I can share my knowledge
You will impress your friends
From me sharing my knowledge with you!

Ivars Zucis (10)
Handforth Grange Primary School, Handforth

All About Me

My name is Leo, it means lionheart
I'm football mad, quick on my feet
At school I work hard to make my teachers proud
Everyone's my friend and I'm their friend
At home with my family and pets I like to do
gaming
Libby does too
I am happy, smiley, smart
I am Leo Lionheart!
This is my world
I will protect it!

Leo McDowell (7)
Handforth Grange Primary School, Handforth

In The Summer

I was born in summer,
There's lots of things to do,
I see the wonderful sun and sea,
The wonderful ice cream looks so good!
I hear the waves crashing down on the shore,
The laughing of children splashing, having fun.
I feel the ice cream cone pattern,
I whizz my hand in the sea.
My feelings are all mixed.

Megan Fields (8)
Handforth Grange Primary School, Handforth

Me And My Best Friend

M y best friend is
E xtraordinary

A nd kind
N onetheless, she is funny
D o you want a best friend like

P oppy?
O h, you need to work for her
P oppy is amazing and came over for a
P arty sleepover
Y es, she is a human.

Medisa Karimpoor (9)
Handforth Grange Primary School, Handforth

This Is Me!

When the sharpest words wanna cut me down,
I'm gonna send some joyfulness.
I'm gonna be the bravest girl in town.
I am smart.
This is me!

Look up, here I come,
Bouncing to the sporty drum.
I am talented and will be seen,
I am funny and kind.
This is me!

Kayla Bhaskar (9)
Handforth Grange Primary School, Handforth

All About Me - The Alfie D Rap

Hey you, look at me,
I'm the rhyme master, Alfie D.
I love drawing monsters and doodles,
I've got a dog, crossed Labrador and Poodle.
I have family living all over the place,
I love storing stuff in my pencil case.

That's all about me
Alfie D!

Alfie Diamond (9)
Handforth Grange Primary School, Handforth

My Likes

There are things about me,
I'd like to share,
I like reading, I like art,
I am always happy,
And I like to play,
With my friends all day,
In the shining sun,
But when it rains,
We say our goodbyes,
And play the next day.

Iris Baird (10)
Handforth Grange Primary School, Handforth

Theo

T heo busts amove
H e can't stop
E ven in bed
O verrated dancing

T oo much dancing
A t birthdays
R eally good at dancing
U sed dance moves
S erenade me.

Theo Tarus (11)

Handforth Grange Primary School, Handforth

My Funny Friend Poem

I love chocolate
You love chocolate
I love to play
We both love to dance
We prance and dance
I love my fabulous, funny friend
We love each other
I go everywhere my friend goes
Friends are a precious gift.

Olivia Neve Bibby (10)
Handforth Grange Primary School, Handforth

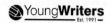

All About Me!

I love chocolate
Bunnies Bob and Oreo
School I like
Friends I enjoy having

Partying is my thing
Fashion with a passion
Swimming is my game
Poppy is my name!

Poppy Lyons (10)
Handforth Grange Primary School, Handforth

Football And Family

I like football, reading and sport,
I also like tennis on the tennis court,
I love my family, they are always so caring.

With my brother I mostly have fun,
And we have loads of laughs on our family run.
I love doing stuff with my mum for fitness,
Baking lime pie and enjoying its richness.

I love football, I play it 24/7,
And on the first of March I will be 11.
My favourite animal is a tiger,
When I play football I'm a striker.

My favourite food is my mum's homemade pizza,
And I loved the holiday when I went to Ibiza.
I like playing football with my cousin,
And when it's raining we go in.

I like to have a laugh,
But getting to my football training can be a faff.
I like football cards and Lego,
But sometimes when I step on it I get a sore toe.

Rory Scott (10)
Kinross Primary School, Kinross

All About Me

Hi, I'm Lucy, I'm five feet tall,
I like to play violin, swimming and netball.
I love to eat my granny's apple pie,
I'm kinda funny and sensible (but only when I try).

I have a dog nicknamed King Barnabus the First,
And I love to read so much I think I might burst!
I like to bake brownies with my sister, dad and
mum,
But when they are all cooked we only have some.

I have a little sister, we share similarities,
But I'm also clumsy, I have a lot of calamities!
I like to do arts and craft, I also like to paint,
I like to do shading from dark to faint.

I like to do cycling and go on hill walks,
I also spot birds, from sparrows to hawks.
I play with neighbours, games to races,
But sometimes I trip over my laces.

Going to the park is a thing I like to do,
Going on roller coasters and going to the zoo.

My friends make me laugh a big belly chuckle,
My family make me smile broad and 'muckle'.

Lucy Young (10)

Kinross Primary School, Kinross

About Me

I am Eilidh Cornwall, here's my poem from me
to you,
These are some things I like to do.
Family walks with my little puppy Fern,
Doing chores in the house for money I earn.
I like to do my weekly dance and swimming,
Doing competitions and galas, mostly winning.
Sometimes I make cookies and cake,
Then maybe fix a mistake or two I make.
Another thing I like is exercise and fitness,
I also like drawing and art,
Loving and enjoying the entire part!
The thing I love most is my family,
All of us spending time together happily.
Nice family dinner we all enjoy,
Saturday game nights, girls vs boys.
Sometimes I call my friends my 'other halfs',
We also like having a carry-on and a laugh.
Weekly sleepovers and going to the park,
Movie nights when it's dark.

By now you have probably learnt a lot about me,
But now I must go for my tea!

Jack Cornwall (11)

Kinross Primary School, Kinross

FIFA With My Stepdad

Playing football with my brother
Playing FIFA
FIFA with my friends
Friends and me playing football
Football is a hobby
Football is me
Me and my mum baking together
Me and my sister watching a movie
Movie night, me and my mum
Movie nights are so fun
Fun is my personality
Fun is calling with my friends
Friends and me at the park
Friends and me eating chocolate
Chocolate is fine for me
Chocolate is sugary enough for me
You and me listening to music
You and me calling
Calling my friends is fun
Calling my dad is joyful
Joyful just like me

Joyful just like eating cheese
Cheese on a sandwich, mmm
Cheese as soft as chicken
Chicken in yummy fajitas
Chicken wings at KFC with my stepdad
Stepdad and me playing football
Stepdad and me going on holiday
Holiday...
Football...

Zac Cormack (10)
Kinross Primary School, Kinross

Boredom With Mum

Calling friends, having fun
Calling friends because of boredom
Boredom makes me play video games
Boredom makes me sleepy
Sleep makes me want my bed
Sleepy makes me warm
Warm has me up all night
Warm has me comfy
Comfy makes me lazy
Comfy has me on my phone
Phone has games
Phone makes me happy
Happy as my nephew smiling
Happy makes me feel bright
Smiling makes me laugh
Smiling to see my favourite food
Food makes my mouth water
Food has me full as balloons
Balloons floating around
Balloons at my family's parties
Parties having a blast

Parties make me laugh
Laugh at my auntie because she's being silly
Silly and being daft playing board games
Silly and dumb with my mum
Mum has me laughing
Mum and me playing Mario Kart.

Nadine Gray (10)
Kinross Primary School, Kinross

Football Before Lasagne

Harris loves sport
Harris loves football
Football is my sport
Football is the best sport
Sport is fun
Sport is good for your legs
Legs in sport are important
Legs make you run
Running is me
Running is good for me for football
Football is my life
Football is active
Active is what I do
Active makes me play with my brother
Brother likes me
Brother is fun
Fun is my thing
Fun helps me with my family
Family loves me
Family helps me calm
Calm helps me relax

Calm makes my brain hungry
Hungry is my thing
Hungry means I need food
Food is good like turkey
Food is good like lasagne
Lasagne is what I like
Lasagne is my favourite
Favourite friend is Charlie P
Favourite friend is Charlie T.

Harris McKenzie (10)

Kinross Primary School, Kinross

Mum And Animals

I like games
I like Mum
Mum makes puzzles with me
Mum like Dad
Dad plays games with me
Dad likes my art
Art is good when you colour
Art is fun like video games
Games like Knack are fun
Games make action figures
Action figures are things I love
Action figures are based on movies
Movies I like are Spider-Man and Ghostbusters
Movies are good like sports
Sports like basketball are fun
Sports I like are running
Running on my treadmill
Running is fun
Fun with my pet
Fun changing my look
Looks on my face are freckles

Blue and sparkly eyes
Eyes are beautiful like hair
Hair is brown and short
Hair is cool like animals
Animals like pandas are cool
Animals are very cute
Cute...
Cool...

Murray Reilly (10)
Kinross Primary School, Kinross

Love Cuddling Friends

Cuddling my cats
Cuddling is love
Love me because of my personality
Love me because I am funny
Funny, I am also smart
Funny and smart, I like to clean
Clean and organising is what I like
Cleaning is what I do with my mum
Mum and Dad and Vincent too
Mum is the best
Best things are what I do
Best holidays with family
Family game night too
Family is fun and caring
Caring to my friends
Caring about my hair
Hair is brown
Hair is straight
Hair is cool
Hair is fun
Fun things I like to do

Fun piano is my favourite
Favourite thing I like to do is dancing
Favourite thing I like is athletics
In athletics I go really fast
At athletics I have friends
Friends are trusting
Trusting and nice.

Edie Taylor (10)
Kinross Primary School, Kinross

All About Me

Hello, I'm Emilie and I have a pet cat
Her name is Islay and she likes to have a nap
Islay likes to run around crazy
Although she's a little dazy.

All my friends are hilarious
But they sometimes are furious
All my friends like to know what I did the weekend before
Me and Masie have lots of play days, but mostly ask for more.

I love to munch on lots of snacks like macaroons
Sometimes I wish there were more moons
I like to imagine I'm in space with a big block of cheese
One time I was eating cheese then I sneezed.

You know already my name is Emilie and I have a pet cat
I like to pretend I'm my mum and put on a funny hat

Me and my mum like spending time with each other
And we both love our bed covers.

Emilie Verdot (10)
Kinross Primary School, Kinross

Fun Playing Piano

Caitlin the girl
Caitlin loves drawing
Drawing is fun
Drawing animals
Animals reading books
Animal programmes on TV
TV murder mysteries
TV, favourite show is 'Friends'
Friends play tig in the playground
Friends hang out at school
School is where I learn
School is where I play basketball
Basketball is fun
Basketball keeps me fit
Fit playing hockey
Fit badminton at weekends
Weekends playing tennis
Weekends spent baking
Baking cookies
Baking with my sister
Sister is annoying

Sister's not like me
Me and Dad do sports
Me and Mum do reading at home
Home is in Kinross
Home makes me happy
Happy playing piano
Happy eating fish and chips
Chips...
Piano...

Caitlin Fenna (11)
Kinross Primary School, Kinross

Happy As Me

Hugo the rugby player
Hugo loves tennis
Tenni on a Monday
Tennis is fun
Fun reading 'Murder on the Orient Express'
Fun in Malta
Malta is historic
Malta has great food
Food like oysters for dinner
Food is my favourite
Favourite shop is the Lego store
Favourite sport is rugby
Rugby is fun
Rugby makes me happy
Happy is when I'm with my dogs
Happy when I am with my family
Family that love me
Family that is kind to me
Me is the person I like to be
Me will always be active
Active with sport

Active as a rugby player
Player playing a board game
Player for Kinross
Kinross is where I go to school
Kinross is my home
Home with my family
Family...
Love...

Hugo Flinn (10)

Kinross Primary School, Kinross

Simply Having Fun

My name is Maisie and I like to read
I like to make bracelets with my cousin out of
beads
I love having Nerf gun fights with my little brother
We always have fun like no other
I love to watch films on a rainy day
Although not all films are great, I have to say
I love playing netball games
Maybe one day we'll have shirts with our names
I enjoy eating pizza with Finn
Soon the pizza box will be in the bin
I like doing dance shows
We're the best, everyone knows
I love to spend time with my dad and mum
We've had some great times, in fact more than
some
I love to have fun
In the sun
In the playground we like to run
Every day having fun

That was some, now I'm done
This was fun!

Maisie McLean (10)

Kinross Primary School, Kinross

The Love In Me

Emily is my name
Emily, I'll always stay the same
Emily, who likes doing art
Emily, with a big heart

I love doing lots of sports
Which includes tennis on the courts
I do hockey which is lots of fun
But I get hot when I do it in the sun

My mum and dad are awesome
They're as sweet as cherry blossom
I'm a little sister to Annabelle
And big one to Freya as well

When I get home I play guitar
And go to a school that's not very far
I like playing with my friends
When I'm with them the fun never ends

I love my dog called Bea
She makes me merry and happy

My nine chickens are minuscule
But they don't like it when it's cool.

Emily Stobie (10)
Kinross Primary School, Kinross

Sweets At The Weekend

Owen the footballer
Owen likes sweets
Sweets so sweet
Sweets from the shop
Shop for clothes
Shop for games
Games with my friends
Games all day
Day with my friends
Da playing tig
Tig in the playground
Tig out of school
School learning
Schoool thinking
Thinking of my dog
Thinking of my cat
Cat called Star
Cat hunting outside
Outside at the park
Outside on my bike
Bike is black and green

Bike to see my friends
Friends go to the football pitch
Friends at a sleepover
Sleepover at my friend's
Sleepover at the weekends
Weekends go to my dad's
Weekends go somewhere to eat
Eat every night
Eat all the time!

Owen Adams (10)

Kinross Primary School, Kinross

Friends And Others

I am Emma
I am a friend
Friend to all
Friend to loads
Laugh at friends' jokes
Jokes to make
Jokes to say
Say silly words together
Say lots
Lots of jokes to tell friends
Lots to say
Say anything to me
Say anything I'll listen
Listen all day
Listen to others
Others listen to me
Others play with me
With friends as well
With family by my side
Loads of crystals to collect
To make me happy

Happy people make me smile
Happy due to family time
Time goes by when I listen to music
Time goes fast when I play with friends
Friends to play with
Friends to talk to
To make me smile
To make me laugh
Laugh till I burst!

Emma Sangster (10)
Kinross Primary School, Kinross

Life With Matthew

Hi, I'm Matthew, I love to eat,
Burgers, chocolate, cake I can't beat.
Fajitas and macaroons in my belly,
I go lie down and watch some telly.

Football, gymnastics and tennis,
I really am a little menace.
Cooking, playing music, banging the drums,
Until bedtime sadly comes.

I love playing with friends,
Baking and making jokes until it ends.
I love to laugh and play,
When everyone cheers hooray!

My mum is supportive, fun and cool,
And sometimes she likes to go to the pool.
She is friendly and kind,
And has a smart mind.

My dad is tall and skinny,
He laughs a lot when we shimmy!

He tells the jokes,
About other folks.

Matthew Gibb (10)

Kinross Primary School, Kinross

Ewan Being Happy

Ewan the boy
Ewan loves dogs
Dogs make me comfy
Dogs make me happy
Happy playing with my brother
Happy playing basketball
Basketball makes me active
Basketball makes me fit
Fit on my skateboard
Fit on my bike
Bike black and red
Bike going to school
School makes me educated
School is Kinross
Kinross walking my dog
Kinross playing rugby
Rugby tackling
Rugby games
Games playing Jenga
Games of tennis
Tennis with Siobhan

Tennis against my mum
Mum playing Uno
Mum doing baking
Baking Victoria sponge
Baking kit for Christmas
Christmas opening presents
Christmas playing with toys
Toys...
Presents...

Ewan Watson (10)
Kinross Primary School, Kinross

Day Of Amazing

Family having fun
Family going on day trips
Day trips to the beach
Day trips with our dog
Dog playing fetch
Dog eating food
Food at a restaurant
Food while watching movies
Movies with my sister
Movies with snacks
Snacks like pizza
Snacks with Dad
Dad is funny
Dad and me drawing
Drawing makes me smile
Drawing my favourite animals
Animals me and Freya both love
Animals running around the park
Park trips with my friends
Park walks with Mum
Mum and me making cakes

Mum helping me sketch
Sketching all my favourite things
Sketching with Freya
Freya and me having fun
Freya is amazing
Amazing fun with family.

Rosie Given (10)
Kinross Primary School, Kinross

Art Is Surrounded

Isabella the dog owner
Isabella loves art
Art is the best
Art is calming
Calming down my sister
Calming down my brother
Brother called Oli
Brother and sister
Sister is Clara
Sister is cute
Cute, cuddly dog
Cute, loveable dog
Dog is called Loki
Dog is the best
Best time ever
Best people together
Together doing sports
Together sprinting and running
Running in the playground
Running all around
Around the TV

Around with my family
Family is the best
Family are so kind
Kind friends
Kind people surrounded
Surrounded by love
Surrounded by happiness
Happiness...
Love...

Isabella Jackson (10)

Kinross Primary School, Kinross

This Is Me

I have a kind heart
And I love to do art
I have a curious mind
I wonder what else I'll find?

Delicious pizza is so spicy
And at times can be very pricey
Eating salami, it is so hot
Although I do love to eat it a lot

Splashing about in the pool
Is a great way to keep me cool
Comfy in bed reading a story
Or watching a movie about finding Dory

Chatting to my mum
And having lots of fun
Or playing with my brother
Who is like no other

Walking in nature even when it's little
Oh look, I found a thistle

I love looking at pictures of dogs
Even the dogs that chew on logs.

Mia Templar (10)
Kinross Primary School, Kinross

Friends Like Playing

Spending time with family
Spending time with friends
Friends coming round
Friends coming swimming
Swimming in the pool
Swimming I find fun
Fun with my parents
Fun watching movies
Movies are my favourite
Movies with my mum
Mum cheers me up
Mum likes cooking
Cooking dinner
Cooking my lunch
Lunch with my friends
Lunch with my brother
Brother and me get on
Brother is caring
Caring for me
Caring for my family
Family is key

Family I miss
Miss my cousins
Miss my music
Music on Alexa
Music is playing
Playing really loud
Playing in my head
Head...
Loud...

Lexie Crawford (10)

Kinross Primary School, Kinross

Brother And Home

Friends are people
Friends make me happy
Happy is my thing
Happy watching The Olympics
Olympics and Winter Olympics
Olympics are sports
Sports are my thing
Sports make me happy
Happy playing football
Happy in running
Running to school
Running back home
Home is where I live
Home is where I'm happy
Sam the footballer
Sam the brother
Brother to Isla
Brother to Alex
Alex is small
Alex is fun
Fun with friends

Friends all around me
Friends make me happy
Happy playing board games
Happy with family
Family and food
Family and friends
Happy...
Love...

Sam Thwaites (10)

Kinross Primary School, Kinross

Fun

I'm Andrew
I'm fun
Fun parents
Fun sisters
Sisters are kind
Sisters are nice
Nice are my cousins
Nice are my friends
Friends I have sleepovers with
Friends we like karting
Karting is fast
Karting you beat people
People play tennis
People play football
Football is teamwork
Football is one of my hobbies
Hobbies like Nerf guns
Hobbies like sports
Sports make me happy
Sport is athletic
Athletic are my friends

Athletic am I
I am crazy
I like jokes
Jokes make me laugh
Jokes make me funny
Funny is me
Funny are comedians
Comedians...
Me!

Andrew Thompson (10)
Kinross Primary School, Kinross

Dogs Are Life

Georgia the younger sister
Georgia likes dogs
Dogs are great
Dogs are caring
Caring to Oliver
Caring to family
Family helps me
Family is fun
Fun is dance
Fun friends
Friends are funny
Friends are cool
Cool family
Cool dog walks
Walks are full of nature
Walks around Kinross
Kinross my town
Kinross is where I go to school
School is fun
School is all about learning
Learning about China

Learning about health
Health is good
Health in hospitals
Hospital is not fun
Hospital takes over your life
Life is the best
Life is great
Great...
Best...

Georgia Hodge (10)
Kinross Primary School, Kinross

Kaiden Likes Animals

Kaiden the swimmer
Kaiden; tennis player
Player of card games
Player of computer games
Games are good
Games are fun
Fun with my brother
Fun with my dog
Dog needs walks
Dog needs cuddles
Cuddles are warm
Cuddles are kind
Kind is a nice thing to be
Kind is beautiful
Beautiful heart
Beautiful family
Family is good to have
Family cares
Cares about cousins
Cares about brother
Brother is funny

Brother is cool
Cool is being born in Australia
Australia is hot
Australia has cool animals
Animals are my favourite
Animals I like
Like...
Favourite...

Kaiden Moffat (10)
Kinross Primary School, Kinross

Fun Is Basketball

Jack the basketballer
Jack loves sports
Sports are fun
Sports are great
Great talking with others
Great talking with siblings
Siblings can be mean
Siblings can be nice
Nice family
Nice friends
Friends encourage
Friends inspire
Inspire to do better
Inspire to do more
More sports
More basketball practice
Practise my skills
Practise with family
Family trips
Family holidays
Holidays to Spain

Holidays to Lanzarote
Lanzarote is sweaty
Sweaty after sports
Sweaty after basketball
Basketball is fun
Basketball is competitive
Fun...
Competitive...

Jack Cornwall (11)
Kinross Primary School, Kinross

Stuff In My Life

Football is fun
Football is speed
Speed is sports
Speed is basketball
Basketball is hard
Basketball is fun
Fun is playing
Fun is family
Family is supportive
Family is everything
Everything is art
Everything is games
Games are addictive
Games are good
Good is FIFA
Good is happy
Happy when Rangers are winning
Winning is not important
Important schoolwork
Important is hard work
Work is making friends

Work is money
Money is hard work
Money can't buy time
Time is family
Time is valuable
Valuable stuff
Valuable animals
Stuff in my life.

Oscar Stewart (10)

Kinross Primary School, Kinross

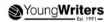

Family And Fun!

Hi, I'm Amy, I like to talk,
And with my dog I like to walk.
I like playing the Roblox game,
I'm always changing my username!

I like to read Dotty Detective,
They really are quite selective.
I like to bake,
Especially cake!

My favourite YouTuber, LDShadowlady,
It's amazing but can be quite shady.
I love toadstools,
They're so cute and cool.

Me and my family,
Always live happily.
I love to penny board,
The edges are as sharp as a sword.

My home is warm,
And full of popcorn.

My favourite bird is a dove,
Because it's full of love.

Amy Lockhart (10)

Kinross Primary School, Kinross

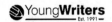

Animals Loving Family

Lily is sporty
Lily likes animals
Animals are cute
Animals are big and small
Small and outgoing
Small and brave
Brave and shy
Brave and calm
Calm when dancing
Calm when reading
Reading books in bed
Reading outside
Outside growing plants
Outside playing
Playing with my sister
Sister is crazy
Sister likes to sing
Sing while listening to music
Sing in the car
Car to McDonald's
Car journey to holidays

Holidays to see family
Holidays to have fun
Fun friends
Fun family
Family is love
Love is in hearts
Hearts...
Love...

Lily Forbes (10)
Kinross Primary School, Kinross

The Things I Love

Swish!
Pretty paint pattering patterns on paper
Mixing colours is as relaxing as sleeping.

Splash!
Basketballs as bouncy as bunnies
Cycling is as exhilarating as swimming.

Stir!
Mum baking brilliant brownish bits of bread
The cakes as fluffy and soft as clouds.

Plop!
Sizzling Super Noodles slither down my throat
The soup as red as tomatoes, the tofu as white as
paper.

Laa!
Marvellous melodies made of many notes
Quavers as short as ants, minims as long as a
trumpet.

Rustle!
Fabulous, fantastic, fun, fascinating facts
Books as breathtaking as nature.

Isabella Chen (10)
Kinross Primary School, Kinross

Kind And Caring

Pets super soft
Pets very kind
Kind little sister
Kind parents
Parents very loving
Parents super loyal
Loyal friendships
Loyal, beautiful horses
Horses I ride
Horses I love
Love going swimming
Love playing games
Games on my tablet
Games on my phone
Phone my gran
Phone my friends
Friends kind to me
Friends asking where am I
I have brown hair
I have earrings
Earrings of different shapes

Earrings that are beautiful
Beautiful drawings
Beautiful mum
Mum is kind
Mum is caring
Caring dad
Caring family
Family is kind.

Kayla Grieve (10)

Kinross Primary School, Kinross

Key To Life

I am a sister
I am a friend
Friend forever
Friend having fun
Fun with everyone
Fun doing baking
Baking yummy cakes
Baking my favourite cookies
Cookies are fun to make
Cookies are tasty
Tasty food
Tasty drinks
Drinks are refreshing
Drinks are cold
Cold is like winter
Cold is refreshing in summer
Summer is fun
Summer is a good time
Time spent with friends
Time spent with pets
Pets are loving

Pets are always there for you
You are helpful
You are kind
Kind and respected
Kind is key
Key to a positive future
Key to life

Millie Hinton (10)

Kinross Primary School, Kinross

Friend

I am a sister
I am a friend
Friends forever
Friend to all
All into swimming
All swimming galas
Galas and competitions
Galas are fun
Fun being tall
Fun having glasses
Glasses on my face
Glasses help my eyes
Eyes are very blue
Shining, fluffy Labrador
Shining sun on dog walks
Walks with my family
Walks with my sister
Sister time together
Sister fun
Fun on holiday
Fun horse riding

Riding and cantering
Riding and playing
Playing with friends
Playing and baking
Baking cakes
Cakes make me happy
Happy...
Cakes...

Anna Jackson (10)

Kinross Primary School, Kinross

Sister Is Hyper

Molly the athlete
Molly the sister
Sister to Callum
Sister kind and happy
Happy around me
Happy with family
Family is kind
Family is loving
Loving dad
Loving mum
Mum's amazing
Mum's the best
Best people with me
Best ever pets
Pet is called Rosie
Pet is called Willow
Willow is hyper
Willow is fun
Fun is everywhere
Fun making cakes
Cakes are big

Cakes are yummy
Yummy chicken nuggets
Yummy delicious sweets
Sweets are sugary
Sweets make me hyper
Hyper all the time
Hyper all night
Night...
Time...

Molly McElroy (10)
Kinross Primary School, Kinross

Active Is Cool

Max like playing outside
Max is active
Active is running
Active is sporty
Sporty is doing sports
Sporty keeps you healthy
Healthy is eating fruit
Healthy is keeping fit
Fit can make you fast
Fit helps you grow
Grow plants
Grow in nature
Nature is wildlife
Nature is animals
Animals are fast
Animals are cute
Cute like my rabbit
Cute cousins
Cousins are fun
Cousins are loud
Loud cars

Loud Max
Max likes animals
Max likes cars
Cars are fast
Cars look cool
Cool animals
Cool movies
Movies...
Animals...

Max Ross (10)
Kinross Primary School, Kinross

Sister Being Active

Erin the class prefect
Erin the sister
Sister to Grace
Sister, kind and caring
Caring is nice
Caring to family
Family fun
Family laughs
Laughs are fun
Laughs are happiness
Happiness is good
Happiness is friendly
Friendly is kind
Friendly is friends
Friends are fun
Friends are kind
Kind is nice
Kind is baking
Baking is fun
Baking is creative
Creative is designing

Designing is fun
Designing is my hobby
Hobbies are fun
Hobbies are active
Active is running
Active is swimming
Running...
Swimming...

Erin Perry (10)
Kinross Primary School, Kinross

This Is Me!

When I see macaroni cheese
I feel so pleased
I absolutely love the cakes
That my parents like to bake

My guitar makes a lovely strum
It has the beat of a drum
I love craft and arts
I construct with different parts

My chickens are very cute
And my dog is too
My little cheeky cat
Runs about the mat

People think I'm funny
I love it when it's sunny
I am always happy
I am very chatty

My family are very funny
They are as sweet as honey

I love my family very much
They are such a lovely bunch!

Nancy Mould (10)
Kinross Primary School, Kinross

Family And Cars

I have friends
I have family
Family is everything
Family is nurturing
Nurturing teachers
Nurturing friends
Friends are kind
Friends are wise
Wise parents
Wise teacher
Teacher is smart
Teacher is joyful
Joyful neighbours
Joyful pets
Pets are small
Pets are fun
Fun races
Fun games
Games are cool
Games are addictive
Addictive pizza

Addictive landmarks
Landmarks are big
Landmarks are popular
Popular activities
Popular cars
Cars are fast
Cars are awesome
Awesome and fast!

Nathan Neve (10)

Kinross Primary School, Kinross

Dogs Are Great

Samuel is my name
Samuel likes dogs
Dogs messing around
Dogs having fun
Fun with friends
Fun with family
Family meeting friends
Family is great
Great at school
Great at home
Home is great
Home is Kinross
Kinross is fun
Kinross is happy
Happy family
Happy life
Life is fun
Life is amazing
Amazing cousins
Amazing uncles
Uncles chatting

Uncles laughing
Laughing friends
Laughing in water
Water at home
Water is great
Great fun
Great family
Family...
Fun...

Samuel Wells (10)
Kinross Primary School, Kinross

Games And Movies

Alfie the skater
Alfie loves games
Games are cool
Games are fun
Fun with friends
Fun forever
Forever me
Forever Alfie
Alfie the gamer
Alfie the brother
Brother to Molly and Isaac
Brother is kind
Kind is good
Kind family
Family and friends
Family is nice
Nice pizza
Nice burgers
Burgers with beef
Burgers to share
Share love

Share kindness
Kindness you need
Kindness to see
See films
See movies
Movies that are fun
Movies that are good
Good...
Fun...

Alfie Barnes (10)

Kinross Primary School, Kinross

Things I Like

Zoom!
Running in races
As fast as the wind

Boom!
Music, melodies make magic moments
Violins as loud as a lion's roar

Hahaha!
Marvel movies with my family
Mum hugs as amazing as me

Mmmm!
Milk and McDonald's makes me happy
Steak pie, as good as reading books

Swoosh!
Blue, big eyes
Blonde long hair as long as a giraffe's neck

Sigh!
Some sleepovers and swimming fun
Friends together as tight as birds flock.

Emma Thompson (10)
Kinross Primary School, Kinross

All About Me

Wow!
Siblings tease themselves on trips
As much energy as a battery

Whoosh!
Serving and smash drop at Sunday tennis
As clever as a drawing

Splash!
Goldfish in a golden glass tank
As golden as a stack of gold

Zoom!
Super speedy and short personality
As fast as a car

Boom!
Midnight snacks, most marvellous movies
As fun as the arcade

Swish!
Cycling across the countryside
Loch Leven, as big as the Amazon forest.

Oliwia Wleklinska (10)
Kinross Primary School, Kinross

This Is Elizabeth!

Squeak!
Smiling, scurrying, squeaking
Nibbling at the bars like they have never been fed

Whoosh!
Running, racing, recognition
Sprinting as fast as lightning

Clip-clop!
Fun, fast, fabulous
Galloping off in the hills like I have never been outside before

Rush!
Busy, best, business
Keeping busy like a bee

Ssshh!
Silent, sly, smart
Quiet as a mouse

Whoop!
Kind, caring, careful
Family as caring as a mother horse.

Elizabeth Flynn (10)
Kinross Primary School, Kinross

This Is Me

Chomp!
Tempura chicken for tea
As crispy as fresh snow

Clip-clop!
Horses are happy on a hack
As happy as a Labrador

Pop!
Strawberry-blonde hair says Eilidh
As orange as Irn Bru

Hahaha!
Fun family and friends
As kind as an elephant

Chop!
Tent pegs to hold down our tent
Blowing winds as cold as ice

Swish!
My mellow fish Marmalade
As sweet as honey.

Eilidh McAleese (10)
Kinross Primary School, Kinross

This Is Me

Goal!
Fun, friendly, frightening football
I am as glued to football as a sheet to a jotter

Woof!
Licky, leaping Luna
Luna is a dog as fluffy as a blanket

Chomp!
Super surprising steak
Steak as juicy as an orange

Charlie!
Brothers being bonkers
Brothers as loud as a foghorn

Huh huh huh!
Rocky, rickety running
Running as fast as The Flash.

Charlie Penny (10)
Kinross Primary School, Kinross

This Is Me

Splash!
Warm water washing around me
Going as fast as a shark

Woof! Woof! Woof!
Loving little rascals my dogs are
As smart as Dogstein

Bong! Bong! Bong!
Big ball bouncing in the air
As much as a hurt bird

Chew! Chew! Chew!
Eating early even more
Eating more than a hungry pig!

Jamie Drummond (10)
Kinross Primary School, Kinross

This Is My Life

My wish is to catch fish
I would cook the fish
I would put it in a dish

I like
To go on a hike
On my bike

A farm
Is like an alarm
The noise of a farm
Is my morning alarm!

Logan Wallace (10)
Kinross Primary School, Kinross

Nessa And I

I have a naughty puppy, her name is Nessa
But I call her Vanessa
She likes to play fetch
But I like to stretch
Nessa likes to bite
And likes to play fight
But sometimes she gives me a fright
When she's wet she smells odd
I go to dry her and give her a nod
She barks a lot so I give her a treat
But then she tries to bite my feet
I adore her little black fluffy face
And her eyebrows too
Even though she likes to poo!
At night-time I cuddle her in tight
She licks my cheek and the little sneak falls asleep!

Mia Booton (8)
Pantside Primary School, Newbridge

What Makes Me

Furry friends and lots of hugs
Dress-up fun and watching funny movies,
Drinking cocoa from a mug
What makes me

A win on my favourite adventure game
The thrill when I see my name
What makes me

Cuddling my pups and throwing their ball
Laughing at them running down the hall
What makes me

Up at the crack of dawn
Waking my mum with a voice like a foghorn
What makes me

I'm happy with the things I've got
And I don't worry about what I've not

That makes me.

Layla May Fritter (10)
Pantside Primary School, Newbridge

My Dream Career

I could be a pilot, lawyer, plumber or artist,
But there's one job that caught my eye...
A chef! You're probably wondering why...
I could make lots of tasty food,
Dinner, desserts and breakfast too,
Always cooking something new,
Hoping that I will have a big queue!
Making snacks, lunch and drinks,
This really does make me think,
What is your dream career?
You can be anything you want to be,
So go on, let's see!

Kira Taylor (11)
Pantside Primary School, Newbridge

All About Me!

D etermined to succeed
A mbitious to become a scientist
N oisy sometimes when I talk and sing
C aring and loving to my family and friends
E nergetic during my dance lessons

M ove around dancing sometimes when I shouldn't
U pbeat classmates and friends
S miley most of the time
I ndependent and hard-working
C lown around sometimes for a laugh!

Shane Thomas (9)

Pantside Primary School, Newbridge

Someone I Love

They are the same gender as my mum
I am her number one fan
2020 was a rubbish year
But I know she is not far from here
Even when my life was rough
She made it not so tough
Even though she left me with love
I now look up and see doves
As strong as she was it's now in me
In my heart she will always be
In her older days she was very wise
Now she is an angel in the sky.

Emily Rush (10)
Pantside Primary School, Newbridge

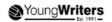

Happiness And All About Me!

To tell you about me
Firstly you have to be happy
Happy to be me
Is being near the sea
It's the sand and the sea that's everything to me
Fair rides are also happiness for me
I smile when I dance
So please come dance and smile with me
I smile with my mum all the time
She smiles with me, that is our life
We are as happy as we can be
Always smile and be happy.

Peyton Beach (8)
Pantside Primary School, Newbridge

Inspiration

I am proud of being a big brother
N ever give up on your dreams
S upporting others
P laying sports with my friends
I ncluding everyone
R ugby makes me happy
A lways be kind
T hink about your actions
I want to be a fireman when I grow up
O utside playing makes me happy
N ever stop being yourself.

Logan Roscoe (9)

Pantside Primary School, Newbridge

This Is Me

This is me, Nathan
I like red, orange and black
Favourite colours

This is me, Nathan
I like toy guns and rifles
Wargaming is fun

This is me, Nathan
I want to be a scientist
I like chemicals

This is me, Nathan
I like the environment
I want to save it

This is me, Nathan
I love all my family
They are all the best.

Nathan Carless (7)
Pantside Primary School, Newbridge

Just Me

I dig all day and mine all night
Nothing but video games and food in my sight
When it's dinner time, pizza is all I need
With lashings of pepperoni and loaded with cheese
In school I have a blast with my friends
At break playing dodgeball, ducking and weaving,
we never want the fun to end
Back at home with my family we laugh together
And it's always a great time.

Jayden Manning (11)
Pantside Primary School, Newbridge

Adjusting

A djusting has been hard for me
D ifferent rules because of Covid
J ust as I start to get used to it
U p early, I get dressed for school
S tressed I feel already
T ough the changes have been
I n and out of isolation
N o one sees how hard it is for me
G oing through these changes, adjusting is hard for me.

Harrison Brown (8)
Pantside Primary School, Newbridge

This Is Me And I Like Coins

C oins are made of kinds of metal

U SA use dollars instead of pounds

R ussia uses ruble instead of pounds

R omania uses leu instead of pounds

E stonia uses euros instead of pounds

N epal uses Indian rupees instead of pounds

C ambodia uses Cambodian riels instead of pounds

Y emen uses rials instead of pounds.

Kai Davies (10)

Pantside Primary School, Newbridge

Things I Like And Things I Don't

I'm dinosaur mad! I've got Lego sets, books and toys
Dinosaurs are not just for boys!

I like playing with friends, watching films and singing rocks
I don't like snakes but I love smelly socks!

I love animals and my family
Reading and playing games
I sometimes have crazy dreams
And I really don't like green beans!

Carys Jones (9)
Pantside Primary School, Newbridge

A Precious Gem

R is for ruby, a precious gem
U is for unique, that's me!
B is for beauty that shines within
Y is for youthful, as young as can be

R is for rose, a beautiful flower
O is for overly helpful, that's me!
S is for super, super at computers
E is for everyone needs a friend.

Ruby-Rose Martin (9)
Pantside Primary School, Newbridge

My Name Is...

A is for active, clever and bright
M is for merry, full of joy
Y is for young dream to achieve

S is for sensible to do the right thing
M is for music, dancing is fun
I is for inquisitive, a curious mind
T is for tingly, always excited
H is for happiness, smiles I give.

Amy Smith (11)
Pantside Primary School, Newbridge

This Is Me

I'm 11 and Shay is my name
In my spare time I like to game
Science and maths I enjoy the most
And I'm head boy, but I don't like to boast
I have a dog named Bea
She loves the beach and the sea
That's all you're getting, I'm out of time
And that's how I'm ending this little rhyme!

Shay Mason (11)
Pantside Primary School, Newbridge

All About Me

O kay, let's talk about me

S mart like an elephant, did you know they have huge brains?

C aring like my mummy, she gives awesome cuddles

A nd I am pretty funny. No

R eally let me tell you a joke

What song do you give for someone's birthday?
Gift rap!
Boom!

Oscar Lewis-Gamble (7)
Pantside Primary School, Newbridge

Skye's World

My name is Skye and I have long hair
To brush, it is a nightmare

My favourite colour is pink
Most girls like the colour I think

I have one sister and one brother
Sometimes we are noisy, my poor mother!

I have two dogs that are very yappy
When I am sad I play with them to make me
happy.

Skye Dugmore (7)
Pantside Primary School, Newbridge

About Me!

I talk all day, arts and crafts all night
Now there are games in my sight
I play my games and talk all the time
I play until night arrives
I love my games, I love my arts
I love my food, space and family
I won't forget my favourite of all...
The colour blue!

Brooke Kavanagh (11)
Pantside Primary School, Newbridge

Family

F ar walks and day trips to the sea
A lways smiling and happy, my family and me
M aking memories to last forever
I n rain or shine having fun together
L ove them now for all of time
Y ou love yours and I love mine.

Casey Jones (10)
Pantside Primary School, Newbridge

All About Marcus

M e and my family love animals
A nimals are cute, cuddly and amazing
R oblox is fun
C uddles from my mum are nice
U nlike other people, we have 26 pets!
S un is fun when you're at the beach.

Marcus Phillips (10)

Pantside Primary School, Newbridge

This Is Me And I Like Superheroes

M ysterio can shoot green fog

A ntman can shrink or grow

R onin wears a ninja suit

V ision protests an Infinity Stone

E lectro fires electricity from his hands

L oki is the god of mischief.

Tylan Davies (9)

Pantside Primary School, Newbridge

The Footballer

I play for Crumlin, it's loads of fun
We all run to score a home run
When our opponents come
We try to make it fun
But all we want to do is beat them
My boots get muddy
My parents don't think it's funny!

Harvey Thomas John Price (9)
Pantside Primary School, Newbridge

This Is Me

My name is Talisha
I'm nine years old
I can be quiet
But my close family and friends know I'm not!
I like making stuff
Big or small
But most of all...
I love my family and all.

Talisha Hughes (9)
Pantside Primary School, Newbridge

This Is Me

C aring and sharing is me
O h how I love to ride my new scooter
R ed is my favourite colour
E gg sandwiches are my favourite
Y ou're lucky to have a friend like me.

Corey Bennett (8)
Pantside Primary School, Newbridge

All About Me

K ind and caring
A eroplanes are my favourite
I magination is cool
D inner time is the best
E ating cooked dinner is delicious
N ight-time is scary.

Kaiden Wheeler (8)

Pantside Primary School, Newbridge

Crisps

C runchy sensation
R eally tasty
I t is my favourite snack
S o I would like some more
P opping flavour in my mouth
S oon the bag will be empty.

Joseph John (7)
Pantside Primary School, Newbridge

All About Me

Swims like a mermaid in the glistening blue sea
Silky, smooth hair
Writing that explodes off the page
Eyes are dark and stormy
Paintings dancing on canvas
Extravagant Eliza!

Eliza Bennett (9)

Pantside Primary School, Newbridge

All About Me

M y favourite colour is blue
Y elling is what I do
L aughing with my friends
E very day in school
S nuggling with Mummy makes me happy at the end.

Myles Challenger (8)

Pantside Primary School, Newbridge

Me And My Life

I like how fast I can run
I want to be a millionaire
When people include me
I am loud, bright and sensitive
A good leader who leads by example
Who shows the way.

Denni Roberts (8)

Pantside Primary School, Newbridge

This Is Me

A pinch of someone who can accept the decision
of the ref
A pinch of someone with care for all his
teammates
A spoonful of someone who cares for his boss and
trainer
A teaspoon of someone who plays fair with no
cheating
A bowl of someone who can listen to a former
player or manager
A spoonful of kindness for his entire team
A chunk of someone who is unique in athletics

Mix a bowl of accepting another person's speech
Even if you think it's silly
Also take a pinch of someone who can accept the
decision of officials
A teaspoon of someone who can play fair
Just to make it a bit more tasty than before
A spoonful of love just for your manager or trainer
A cupful of kindness for all your teammates
Last ingredient of all, someone unique in athletics

Now put it on a tray and put it in the oven at 180 degrees for 30 minutes then take it out
And now you have a pro-athlete.

Daniel Bordon (9)

Pardes House Primary School, Finchley

Mostly Me

Ingredients:
One bag of art
Boxes of books
A bottle of jokes
A tablespoon of maths
26 litres of fun
A lot of Torah
A tweak of Taffys
A few ounces of reading
Some sweets
A few friends
100 more friends
Another 4 litres of fun
Some more sweets
7 sprinkles of English

Method:
First, mix the tablespoon of maths
With the 7 sprinkles of English
Drop some sweets in
Add the boxes of books
Then take the 26 litres of fun

And pour in the bottle of jokes
Shake it well and pour it in
Put a few ounces of reading in
Next, take one bag of art and drop it in
Mix with a tweak of Taffys and a few friends
Use a lot of Torah
And 100 more friends
Add some more sweets
And 4 litres of fun.

There, you're all done!

Yitzi Raymond (10)
Pardes House Primary School, Finchley

My Favourite Author

Mysteries, secrets, plot and schemes,
Books of friends finding out things in teams.
Twins together being sent to a school,
Their crowns were knocked off, they were put
under rule.

A story of a grand four towers,
With girls of all powers.
Sometimes things are sad,
But never end up bad.

It might be a chair, it might be a tree,
It might be a scholarship fee.
Seven friends of boys and girls,
Finding a thief or perhaps a lady's precious pearls.

Four pals and a dog too,
They have an island shared between them and
that's plain true.
These books always get better and brighter,
But can you guess the writer?

The author is... Enid Blyton.

Avi Schleider (10)
Pardes House Primary School, Finchley

My Favourite Book

A battle between good and evil that goes on for
seven years
That includes wizards, witches and house-elves
with pointy ears
The story began on his first birthday
His life started out perfect but was not to stay
His parents were murdered, he was about to follow
And that resulted in him leaving Godric's Hollow
A giant of a man took him to his aunt and uncle's
house
Their names were Vernon and Petunia, his spouse
When he was eleven the giant man returned
And he took him to a school where magic he
learned
Year after year, death he cheated
Until finally The Dark Lord he defeated
If you guessed it you must be a spotter
The book I'm talking about is Harry Potter.

Avraimy Cutler (9)
Pardes House Primary School, Finchley

My Favourite Thing

Painting and colouring is my thing
I'm fast, I will be the first in every race
I like to dance and sing
Bananas are my favourite healthy food

I am very skinny so I need to eat
When I see a dog I want to pet it
When I am hungry I want a sweet
The only subject I will do is maths

When it's summer I want to go to the beach
When I hear a riddle I'll tell it to my friends
I have short arms so I can't reach
I like to do cool tricks on the trampoline

I am short so I can't reach up high
When I get home I like to watch
I am a good boy, I never lie
Sometimes I like to play Monopoly.

Daniel Bude (10)

Pardes House Primary School, Finchley

What I'm Like

To create me you will need:

A golden football that shines like the moon
A bucket of cricket balls
A chocolate bar that is completely smooth
A bookcase of books
A handful of sweets that are super sticky
A pinch of fun
A dash of happiness and mischief

Break up the football, put it in the mixer
Add the bucket of cricket balls
Melt the chocolate then pour on the cricket balls
Add books page by page
Cut up sweets and add to the mixture
Pour in the pinch of fun as quick as a flash
And the dash of happiness and mischief
Finally, bake in the oven till as chewy as a biscuit.

Yissochor Moller (10)

Pardes House Primary School, Finchley

All About Me

A spoonful of joy
A football
A cup of Torah
A bowl full of white chocolate
25 books
An aircraft of sunshine
A handful of snow as cold as ice
A spoonful of peace

Put in the spoonful of joy
Now add the football
Then pour in the cup of Torah
Mix it with the bowlful of chocolate
Now throw in the 25 books
Add the aircraft of sunshine
Put in a handful of snow
Now put it in the oven at 160 degrees
Put in the spoonful of peace
Take out of the oven after 25 minutes.

Yossef Besnainou (10)
Pardes House Primary School, Finchley

My Favourite Subject

To make me you will need:
A selection of art books
A golden canvas
A silver brush
A selection of paint
A diamond palette
A platinum stool

Sit on the diamond stool
Open the golden set of tools
Open a book and begin to sketch
Careful not to squiggle and go out of place
Take out the paint
But don't faint!
Begin to draw
Finally, let it dry
It could be you or me

What am I?

Answer: An artist.

Yisroel Gurvits (10)
Pardes House Primary School, Finchley

Sruli!

S ruli loves ball games
R ound to the shop he goes
U sually has pizza every weekend
L oves chocolate and vanilla ice cream
I s a very trusted boy

S mells of sweets
P lays Gameboy really well
R eally hates the subject English
I s always baking
N ever brushes his teeth
G reat at all subjects
E ven enthusiastic in his worst subject
R eally realistic.

Sruli Springer (8)
Pardes House Primary School, Finchley

Ashi's Poem

A shi is very chilled sometimes I do not like school
S porty person, good at football especially
H e likes any Jewish meat and does not like pasta
I love learning Jewish studies and I am an uncle

K raus is a good name for me which I like
R eally hates swimming in Mill Hill
A lso has a birthday in April
U nbelievably into Jewish music and singing
S tupid maths he hates and English.

Ashi Kraus (9)

Pardes House Primary School, Finchley

My Legendary Life

A loha, nice to meet you
L oves drawing and Minecraft too
L aughing, giggling in the sun

A nd in the soft play having some fun
B ut bananas I hate
O f course, for school I'm late
U K is where my location is at
T ransport is useful and that is that

M inions are the ones who are so cute
E vil Bratt fought Gru for some loot.

Yosef Elmkies (8)
Pardes House Primary School, Finchley

A Terrific Mixture

3 pinches of guitar
1 tablespoon of piano
3 grams of football
8 spoons of chilling
5 chops of basketball
1 cup of tennis

Stir the basketball and football slowly
Mix the piano with the pinches of guitar roughly
Mix the spoons of chilling with the basketball
smoothly
Pour it all together
Put it in the oven for 24 minutes
Take it out and you get...
Me!

Rephael Hakkak (9)
Pardes House Primary School, Finchley

How To Create Me

To create me you will need:
A bag full of friends
Wembley Stadium
A pinch of fun
5 tablespoons of happiness
half a can of passion

Now you will need to:
Fry Wembley Stadium with 5 tablespoons of happiness
Then add a big bag of friends
Next, add the half a can of passion
After that, add the pinch of fun
Finally, put the mixture in the oven for 40 minutes.

Yoni Hoffman (9)
Pardes House Primary School, Finchley

The Recipe For Me

10 teaspoons of curiosity
A bash of independence
A jar of giggly jokes
8 layers of icing for happiness
Sprinkles of creativity
And a cherry of laughter

Once it's in a bowl
Stir for a minute or two
After that, in the oven it goes
130 degrees for thirty minutes
Once that's done, add the icing and sprinkles
With the cherry
Just for you.

Rafi Miller (9)
Pardes House Primary School, Finchley

To Make Me

Ingredients:
A pinch of maths
6 sprinkles of smiles
9 grams of art
8 teaspoons of happiness
A room full of books
A slice of pizza

Method:
Take a bowl and the pinch of maths
Add the 9 grams of art and mix
Add the 8 teaspoons of happiness
Add the slice of pizza with the room of books
Mix all the ingredients.

Zvi Gutfreund (9)
Pardes House Primary School, Finchley

This Is Ben's Poem!

B en likes football, running and swimming

E xercise is very good for you and I like exercise

N aughty is bad, but I like being naughty and silly sometimes!

J umping I like on a trampoline

A shi and Eli are my best friends

M y mummy is so cool

I love football

N anny gives me so much money.

Ben Friedman (10)

Pardes House Primary School, Finchley

This Is Me

T he favourite colour of mine is red
H air colour, dark brown
I am very good at sports, especially football
S mart is what I am

I have three siblings, one girl and two boys
S chool is not my thing

M y friends say I'm popular
E yes as brown as chocolate.

Ben Spitzer (9)
Pardes House Primary School, Finchley

Fun Is Me

F illed with laughter
U mbrellas keep you safe
N aughty and cheeky
N ovellino restaurant is one of the best
Y ummy food

C alm boy
H appy boy
I include other boys
L augh a lot
L ittle boy
E ggs are yummy
D rink a lot.

Oshi Levy (10)
Pardes House Primary School, Finchley

What King Am I?

This is the year of the Great Fire of London
Samuel Pepys wrote in a diary in my reign
Sir Issac Newton discovered gravity
The year before was a plague
My father was Charles I
My brother was the Duke of York
I brought back the Crown Jewels
Did you get me?

Answer: I'm Charles II.

Eli Mordfield (9)
Pardes House Primary School, Finchley

I Love Food

C arrots, cucumbers and cauliflower I dread

H ot dogs and chips make my stomach not hungry

I eat lots of food like a gorilla

L ollipops and crisps I adore

L affy Taffys are very sticky

E ncore's is my favourite chocolate

D oughnuts can make me fat!

Chaim Ackerman (10)

Pardes House Primary School, Finchley

The Colour That I Like

The colour that I like is the same colour as the sky
It is the same colour as the sea
It's a wonderful colour that most boys like
The colour can come as a school shirt
It can be a dark or light colour
It's the colour of our school lockers.
What is it?

Answer: Blue.

Dovid Greenberg (10)
Pardes House Primary School, Finchley

Ariel's Poem

H opping and jumping is my thing
A riel will become king
P opping bags I like
P laying football is my hobby
Y ummy pizza is good for me

B lowing balloons I don't know how to
O riginal I am
Y ellow is my favourite colour.

Ariel Weissbraun (9)
Pardes House Primary School, Finchley

It's Me!

It's me, it's me, the famous me
The funniest me, the best of me
I like potatoes but hate tomatoes
You'll never find one on my plate
Because that's the vegetable I just hate!
I love big brown bears
The way they roar and the way they stare!

Aaron Winegarten (8)
Pardes House Primary School, Finchley

How You Make Me

As handsome as a handsome prince
Put a cup of excitement in
A tablespoon of curiosity
A room full of books
20 comics
A dash of sadness
Half a cup of happiness
A sprinkle of pizza
Mix altogether
And cook for 20 minutes
That makes me!

Kovi Diamant (8)
Pardes House Primary School, Finchley

All About Shimeon

My name is Shimeon
And I am very clever!
My brain is as big as a house
I am as fast as a lion
I am also very happy
My favourite food is pizza
My hobby is champ (ball game) and hand tennis
My second favourite food is ice cream and chips.

Shimeon Israeli (8)
Pardes House Primary School, Finchley

Tuvia

T uvia's my name, fun is my game
U p in the lift you'd find my home
V acuum cleaners are useful for me because
I like to clean with my mummy
A nd I love the world, there's so much to learn.

Tuvia Deutsch (8)
Pardes House Primary School, Finchley

Yossi The Great!

Yossi is an awesome kid
Whose muscles are very big
His football skills are very good
Like a star's skills should
He is as tall as a tree
As tall as can be
His supersonic legs are fast
He could even run to Mars!

Yossi Werjuka (9)
Pardes House Primary School, Finchley

My Favourite Lesson

It's my favourite lesson
It's got colours
It's about artists
And landscape or portrait
You can use paint with pallets
You can use pastels or crayons
And pencils.
What is it?

Answer: Art.

Sruli Hackenbroch (9)

Pardes House Primary School, Finchley

Animals Riddle

As furry as a dog
Small whiskers on its cheek
Jumps like a kangaroo
Fast as a cheetah
Carrots are its food
Likes to be held
Only found on land.
What is it?

Answer: A rabbit.

Ari Lerch (10)
Pardes House Primary School, Finchley

Raphael

R eally ravishing

A bsolutely amazing

P erfect

H ighly humourous

A rticulate

E nthusiastic

L ovely boy.

Raphael Posen (8)

Pardes House Primary School, Finchley

Avi K

A vi is my name

V ictory Line is on the Underground trains

I am alone but I have a bro

K eeping a smile on my face.

Avi Kahan (8)
Pardes House Primary School, Finchley

What I Am

I am as clever as a wizard
And as quiet as a lizard
I am very fast
But I always come last
And I feel like I am in a blizzard!

Izy Benaim (8)

Pardes House Primary School, Finchley

Loves Of My Life

A lways love to play with my brother Avi and make the family laugh!

M y friends think I am a chatterbox, thoughtful, happy and exciting, but I can be quiet and shy with others.

A m a boy of seven years old. When I grow up I want to help others who are in need.

R obin is my mummy and she looks after me and is the kindest person I know.

M y hobbies are football, rock climbing and playing rock music on my electric guitar.

A run is my daddy and he is really funny but sometimes strict with homework.

D on't like rude people, selfish and unkind behaviour towards others.

A spire to be the best I can be and strive to always improve.

H arry Potter is my favourite character that I love to read and watch!

A s for colours, orange is my favourite and fills me with energy and sunshine.

R eally love to see a giant tarantula which is my favourite creature. The feel of it crawling up my arm sends shivers down my spine.

Amar Madahar (7)
St Martin's School, Mill Hill

The Future I Think Of

The future I think of is to compete as an Olympic runner
Chasing towards my dreams and never giving up
No matter how many thoughts get in my way I will never stop
The future I dream of is to become a pilot
Flying free over the world
I'd fly through the clouds along with my problems to free my mind
The future I think of is to move to Japan and become an animator
Using the creativity and colours in my mind
The future I think of is to save the planet
Protect everyone, care for everyone and look out for my family
That is the future I am longing for.

Chloe Barber (11)
St Martin's School, Mill Hill

The Beach

The beach
Children running
Skipping and jumping
Ice cream vans caressing the sand
The sun beaming onto the land
And the trees moving like a band

The salty sea dancing in the breeze
Like bees buzzing on a trapeze

The clouds hanging in the sky like cotton candy
Which can come in handy!

Olivia Wilson (10)
St Martin's School, Mill Hill

I Am A Ticking Time Bomb

I twist and wriggle and squirm, I hate the terms
they use against me
It builds up inside like I'm about to explode
I'm like a toy with what they say, yet I am a jack-in-
the-box
The handle is turning until it's time...
The jumping figure is out... tic!
I can't explain what the feeling is like
But only that I am a ticking time bomb inside
I do not like this, it's draining me out
Every day it gets more challenging
I am trying to hide it, but why should I?
We should not feel ashamed
This tic monster inside just makes me *me!*

Poppy Webb (11)
St Mary's RC Primary School, Lowestoft

A Recipe To Make Me!

A recipe to make me is very hard, because I'm very unique!

To make me you will need
A spoonful of dancing
A cup of drawing
A bottle of designing
And a dream of becoming a fashion designer
100g of piano
And a hint of maths

Stir well!

Baikey Hou (10)
St Mary's RC Primary School, Lowestoft

This Is Me

I am as intelligent as a penguin,
I am amazing at football, I am better than
Raheem Sterling,
I love doughnuts! They are so delicious,
I have a dog, he is the best dog in the whole world,
I have a very annoying sister who is older than me,
I am very clever, just like my older sister,
I am awesome at gaming, I am better than
my sister,
I can swim in the swimming pool,
I will always accept chocolate and sweets!

This is me!

Maia Magson (9)
Thameside Primary School, Caversham

This Is Who I Am!

I am a girl
I love dogs, Beagles are my favourite
I am Evie with my own identity
I am a sister, kind but mostly annoying

I am funny, sarcasm comes naturally
I am sneaky, as sneaky as a mouse
I am a lion, strong and brave
I am a daughter, loyal to my parents

I am a swimmer, growing stronger every day
I am a book, I can answer any question
I love mice, my obsession grows by each hour

This is me.

Evie Titchener (9)
Thameside Primary School, Caversham

Pokémon Fan

I am from China
I am a dragon, quick and swift
I am a Pokémon fan, I collect their cards
I am a brother; helpful and intelligent.

I am a good friend
I help my friends
I am an insect lover, well, not cockroaches
I am a football fan; I play it at school.

I am curious
As curious as can be
I am honest, I tell the truth even if it means I get in trouble.

This is me.

Eason Wu (9)
Thameside Primary School, Caversham

I'm Growing Day By Day

I am Rose, I have questions that can't be solved.
I am a girl, fit and strong.
I am a director, stubborn but fun.
I am popcorn, salty but sweet.
I'm me.

I am a rose, I grow to the sky.
I am a sister, Higleys are the best.
I am a book, I can answer anything.
I am a baker, my secret ingredient is love.
I am an animal lover, I love pigs.
I love pink.

This is me.

Rose Higley (10)
Thameside Primary School, Caversham

Me

I love my parrot, he makes me smile,
With him in my pocket I could walk a mile.
I love the warmth of the smiling sun,
Me and my friends love having fun.
I like to play in the mushy, squishy mud with my friends,
The fun never ends.
My favourite food is macaroni cheese,
Second helping please!
I like to watch the seagulls float, I watch them fly,
Through the azure sky.
This is me!

Aadhya Shukla (9)
Thameside Primary School, Caversham

This Is Me

I am as chatty as a parrot,
I am as fast as a cheetah when I'm late for school,
I am as forgetful as a goldfish at spelling,
I am as funny as a comedian in a circus,
My heart is as red as a ruby,
I'm as kind-hearted as a fairy,
I'm a bookworm in my bed,
I'm as hard-working as a nurse during the pandemic,
My hair is as golden as a lion's mane.

This is me!

Hannah Spencer (10)
Thameside Primary School, Caversham

This Is Me

This is me,
A stealthy fox,
When the moon illuminates
In the starry sky.

This is me,
An optimistic ray of sunshine,
Trying to brighten,
Someone's day.

This is me,
An elastic band,
That bends and twists in various ways,
Gymnastics is my thing.

This is me,
A boisterous beam of light,
Energising dull places.

This is me!

Deanne Gyeni (10)
Thameside Primary School, Caversham

My Identity

I am a daydreamer
I am a lion, with valour and loyalty
I am sporty at gymnastics and basketball
I am a sister, loyal, crafty and intelligent
I am a beautiful person
I am a friend to a friend
I am cool like ice
I play it cool like silent mice
I am helpful to those around me
I am a daughter, fierce and strong
I want to be confident and free
This is me, my identity.

Saida Rahman
Thameside Primary School, Caversham

This Is Who I Am!

I am a girl
I am Indi with my own identity
I am a dancer and singer
I am a sister and a daughter; loyal, kind and funny

I am nice and cool as ice
Strong as a tiger with lots of meat
Understanding, an open book
I am a mystery and nothing gets out of me

Loving animals every minute
With lots of extended family
Need my help, I am here
This is me.

Indi Holland (9)
Thameside Primary School, Caversham

This Is Me

I am a cat lover
I am a leopard, fast and brave
I am an ant, small and scared
I am a collector, Pokémon cards shared

I am obliged
I am a sun, I will always ride
I am a brother, kind but annoying
I am courageous, I do not fear mistakes

I am free
I am caring and loving
I am a son, proud and brave
I am everything, this is *me!*

Ernie Owens (9)
Thameside Primary School, Caversham

All About Me

I am a daydreamer and a food lover
I adore painting the most
And I love going along the coast
I am a student working hard

I am a chatterbox
I always have something to talk about
I am as curious as a cat
And I dislike wearing hats

I am kind
I usually remind others
My favourite colour is turquoise
And that is all about me!

Nadia Ouadahi (9)
Thameside Primary School, Caversham

I Am Myself

I don't want to boast,
But art is the thing I love the most.
My hair is like bark,
But it's not too dark.

I don't believe in ghosts,
I also love walking along the coast.
I am quite silly,
But I don't like being chilly.

I work hard,
And also like to play in the backyard.
I am like popcorn,
Salty but sweet.

Phoebe Hinchmore (10)
Thameside Primary School, Caversham

I Love Dogs

I am a mystery
I am a lion, courageous and dangerous
I am a dog lover, I love my three
On my side I feel free

I am thoughtful
I am helpful to those around me
I am a small sister, but sometimes it's quite
annoying

I am funny, brave and kind
I am as beautiful as a queen
I help others who are in need

This is me.

Mary Mackinnon (9)
Thameside Primary School, Caversham

This Is Me

I am a boy
I am Ben and I am unique
I am sporty and I play football
I am a brother

I am energetic
I am loyal and a good friend
I love football, I support Manchester United
I am a mystery, I do not like to share

I am an animal person, I love dogs
Staffies are my favourite
I take them for walks

This is me.

Ben Martin (9)
Thameside Primary School, Caversham

This Is Me

I am a girl
I am as strong as a gorilla
I am independent, no one can stop me
I am sneaky, like a mouse finding cheese
I am as loyal as a lion
I am a dog lover
I am a sister, kind and annoying sometimes
I am sporty
I am kind
I am as beautiful as a queen
I am in love with sweets
I am emotional
This is me!

Tamzin Biddle (10)
Thameside Primary School, Caversham

This Is Me

I am as brave as a lion
I am as fast as a cheetah
I am as silent as a jaguar in the night
I am as tall as a giraffe
I am as dangerous as a shark
I am as hungry as a pig
I am as big as an elephant
I am as funny as a comedian
I am as healthy as air
I am as shiny as the sun
This is me.

Yavuz Selim Baydu (9)

Thameside Primary School, Caversham

This Is Me

I am fast, as fast as a car,
I am as stealthy as air,
I am a Labrador, patient and loyal,
I never give up because I have the heart of an angel,
My hair is gold, more pure than diamonds,
My heart is red, as red as a warm ruby,
I am something you will never find nor see.

This is me!

Roman Bosklopper (10)
Thameside Primary School, Caversham

I Am...

I am a football fan
I am a Liverpool supporter
I am strong
I am smart
I am loving
I am emotional
I am a leader
I am a Pokémon fan
I am funny and silly
I am honest
I am a brother
I am helpful and kind
I am trustworthy
I am free
I am me!

Jaide Thompson (10)
Thameside Primary School, Caversham

This Is Me!

I am a girl
I am Grace
I am a mystery
I am as loyal as a lion
I am emotional, my mood is dark as the night sky
I am a sister, kind and helpful to my family

I am as bright as the sun
I am a cat mum
I am outdoorsy
I am brave
I am me

This is me!

Grace Hilden
Thameside Primary School, Caversham

This Is Me

I am joyful, as joyful as a ray of sunshine.
This is me, cool and chatty.
I am as intelligent as an undercover Einstein.
I'm talented, acting, dancing and singing, great at those.
My family are loving, kind and supportive.
This is me.

Jake Mackrory (9)
Thameside Primary School, Caversham

This Is Me

I am as fast as a cheetah
I am as boisterous as a hyena
I am as jumpy as a kangaroo
I am as stealthy as air
I am a star striker in football
I love pizza, it's so cheesy
I talk as much as a parrot.

This is me.

Barney Grace (10)
Thameside Primary School, Caversham

This Is Me

I am as speedy as a cheetah
I am great at football
I don't worry about anything
I love chocolate cake
I am as stealthy as a fox
I am as short as a giraffe
I am as chatty as a chatterbox.

This is me!

Hessah Alhouti (9)
Thameside Primary School, Caversham

 Young**Writers**® Est. 1991

YOUNG WRITERS INFORMATION

We hope you have enjoyed reading this book – and that you will continue to in the coming years.

If you're the parent or family member of an enthusiastic poet or story writer, do visit our website **www.youngwriters.co.uk/subscribe** and sign up to receive news, competitions, writing challenges and tips, activities and much, much more! There's lots to keep budding writers motivated!

If you would like to order further copies of this book, or any of our other titles, then please give us a call or order via your online account.

Young Writers
Remus House
Coltsfoot Drive
Peterborough
PE2 9BF
(01733) 890066
info@youngwriters.co.uk

Join in the conversation!
Tips, news, giveaways and much more!

 **YoungWritersUK**  **YoungWritersCW**  **youngwriterscw**